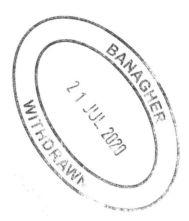
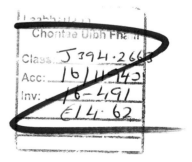

First Facts®

Christmas around the World

Christmas in
MEXICO

by Cheryl L. Enderlein

raintree
a capstone company — publishers for children

Raintree is an imprint of Capstone Global Library Limited, a company incorporated in England and Wales having its registered office at 264 Banbury Road, Oxford, OX2 7DY – Registered company number: 6695582

www.raintree.co.uk
myorders@raintree.co.uk

Christine Peterson, editor; Ted Williams, designer; Eric Gohl, media researcher; Kathy McColley, production specialist

ISBN 978 1 4747 2571 2
20 19 18 17 16
10 9 8 7 6 5 4 3 2 1

British Library Cataloguing in Publication Data
A full catalogue record for this book is available from the British Library.

Acknowledgements
We would like to thank the following for permission to reproduce photographs: AP Images: Eduardo Verdugo, cover; BigStockPhoto.com: holbox, 1; Capstone Studio: Karon Dubke, 21; Dreamstime: Hupeng, 11; Getty Images: LatinContent/Mario Castillo, 17; Newscom: Notimex/ Francisco Santiago, 20, Notimex/Javier Lira, 6, Notimex/Jorge Gonzalez, 8, Notimex/Jose Luis Salmeron, 12, Photoshot/Xinhua/David de la Paz, 15, Zuma Press/El Universal, 5; Shutterstock: Nathalie Speliers Ufermann, 18. Design elements: Shutterstock.

Every effort has been made to contact copyright holders of material reproduced in this book. Any omissions will be rectified in subsequent printings if notice is given to the publisher.

All the internet addresses (URLs) given in this book were valid at the time of going to press. However, due to the dynamic nature of the internet, some addresses may have changed, or sites may have changed or ceased to exist since publication. While the author and publisher regret any inconvenience this may cause readers, no responsibility for any such changes can be accepted by either the author or the publisher.

Made in China

CONTENTS

Christmas in Mexico

Music and children fill the streets. Bright red flowers decorate homes. Welcome to Christmas in Mexico! People around the world celebrate Christmas on 25 December. But in Mexico, holiday celebrations begin on 16 December and end on 2 February. People celebrate Christmas with traditional music, food and religious ceremonies.

How to say it!

In Mexico people say *"Feliz Navidad"*, which means "Happy Christmas".

Mexico

The first Christmas

Christmas is a **Christian** festival celebrating the birth of Jesus. Christians believe that long ago, Jesus' parents, Mary and Joseph, travelled to the town of Bethlehem. The town was crowded, and they had nowhere to stay. They took shelter in a stable. There, Jesus was born. Poor shepherds and rich kings celebrated his birth.

Christian person who follows a religion based on the teachings of Jesus. Christians believe that Jesus is the son of God.

Christmas celebrations

Beginning on 16 December, Mexicans celebrate Christmas with *posadas*. Children go door to door asking for a place to sleep.

posada Christmas festival that plays out Mary and Joseph's search for somewhere to stay

The children carry small figures of Mary and Joseph. When people let them in, children give them the figures. Then everyone celebrates with a feast. Children crack open *piñatas* to get chocolates and gifts.

On Christmas Eve children lead a procession to church. They place a figure of baby Jesus in the church. Families also go to church on Christmas Day.

CHRISTMAS FACT!

After some Christmas Eve services, bells ring out and fireworks light up the sky.

Christmas symbols

Christmas symbols such as poinsettias hold special meaning in Mexico. This plant is part of a Christmas story. A girl wanted to take a gift to church for baby Jesus. But the girl was poor. So she picked some leaves from along the road as a gift. When she put the leaves by Jesus, they turned bright red.

CHRISTMAS FACT!

People call poinsettias *Flores de Noche Buena*. This means "Flowers of the Holy Night".

Christmas decorations

Bright lights and decorations fill homes and cities during Christmas in Mexico. People put out **evergreens**, poinsettias and lilies. They make paper lanterns.

Families set up **nativities** in their homes. This scene includes figures of Mary, Joseph and baby Jesus. It may also include figures of angels, shepherds and animals.

evergreen tree or bush that has green leaves all year round
nativity representation of the birth of Jesus

Santa Claus

Santa Claus is part of the celebrations in Mexico's larger cities. He brings gifts on Christmas Eve.

But for most children, it is the Three Kings who bring presents. These kings brought gifts to Jesus in Bethlehem. In Mexico the Kings bring gifts on 6 January. This day marks the **Epiphany**, the country's main Christmas celebration.

Epiphany Christian festival celebrated on 6 January to mark the Three Kings' visit to baby Jesus

CHRISTMAS FACT!

Saint Nicholas was the first Santa Claus. He secretly gave gifts to children and poor people.

Christmas presents

Imagine your shoes filled with chocolate and gifts. That's what children in Mexico wake up to on 6 January. Before Christmas, children write letters asking the Three Kings for gifts. On 5 January, children put their shoes on a window sill before going to bed. When they wake up, they find their shoes filled with presents from the Three Kings.

CHRISTMAS FACT!

A small figure of baby Jesus is hidden in the bread. Whoever finds the figure must host a party on 2 February.

Christmas food

Tortillas, sweet bread and hot chocolate. Christmas is a delicious time in Mexico. On Christmas Day people enjoy turkey, tortillas and a fruit and vegetable salad. Mexicans make a sweet bread called *Rosca de Reyes* on 6 January. This ring-shaped treat is topped with candied fruit and served with hot chocolate.

Christmas songs

In Mexico children sing special songs during *posadas*. At each house they sing a song asking for a place to stay. Through song, the owner either turns them away or welcomes them inside. Children also sing a lullaby to baby Jesus.

Hands-on:
MAKE A PIÑATA

Children across Mexico celebrate Christmas by making and breaking a *piñata*. You can make a *piñata* for your Christmas party.

What you need

- 1 round balloon
- measuring jug
- 360 millilitres (1½ cups) white glue
- 120 millilitres (½ cup) water
- mixing bowl
- spoon
- newspapers
- red, green and white paint
- string

What to do

1. Blow up the balloon. Ask an adult to help you tie the end.
2. Measure the glue and water. Pour both into a mixing bowl and stir.
3. Tear newspapers into long strips about 5 centimetres (2 inches) wide. Dip a newspaper strip into the glue mixture until it is covered completely.
4. Stick the newspaper strip onto the balloon. Continue adding strips to the balloon until it is covered with three layers of newspaper. Let the newspaper dry.
5. When dry, paint the *piñata* red, green and white – the colours of Mexico.
6. When the paint dries, pop the balloon. Tie a string to the top of the *piñata*. Fill the *piñata* with sweets, toys and small gifts and invite friends to help break it open.

GLOSSARY

Christian person who follows a religion based on the teachings of Jesus. Christians believe that Jesus is the son of God.

Epiphany Christian festival celebrated on 6 January to mark the Three Kings' visit to baby Jesus

evergreen tree or bush that has green leaves all year round

nativity representation of the birth of Jesus

posada Christmas festival that plays out Mary and Joseph's search for lodging

READ MORE

Big Book of Christmas Decorations to Cut, Fold and & Stick, Fiona Watt (Usborne Publishing Ltd, 2013)

Christmas (Holidays and Festivals), Nancy Dickmann (Raintee, 2011)

Mexico: A Benjamin Blog and His Inquisitive Dog Guide (Country Guides), Anita Ganeri (Raintree, 2014)

WEBSITE

www.bbc.co.uk/newsround/15790210

Learn about some more Christmas traditions from around the world.

INDEX